Old Country Road
Vol. 1.

Jose A. Villalba

This book is dedicated to my family and friends, who have always inspired my art and creativity.

Thank You, JV

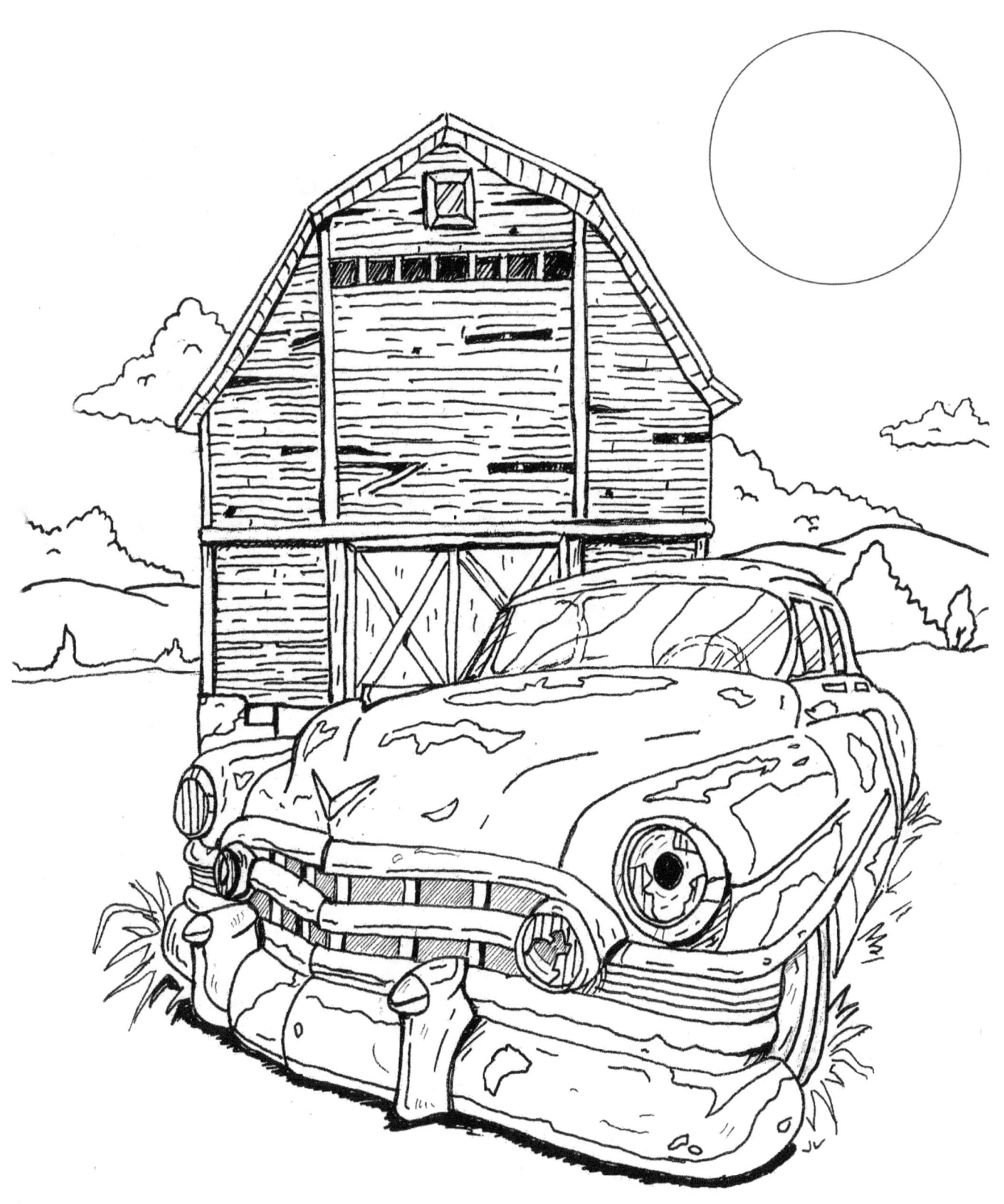

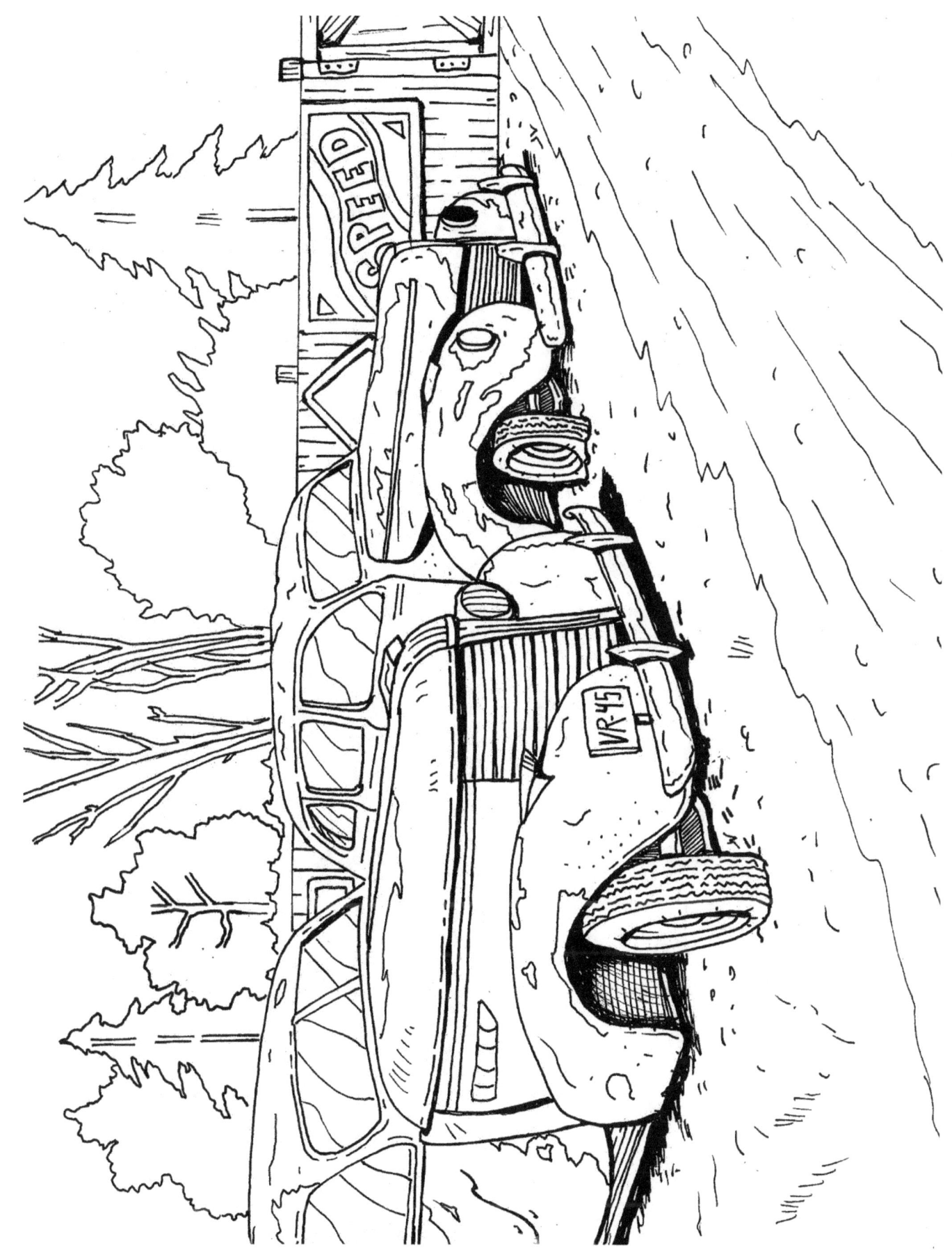

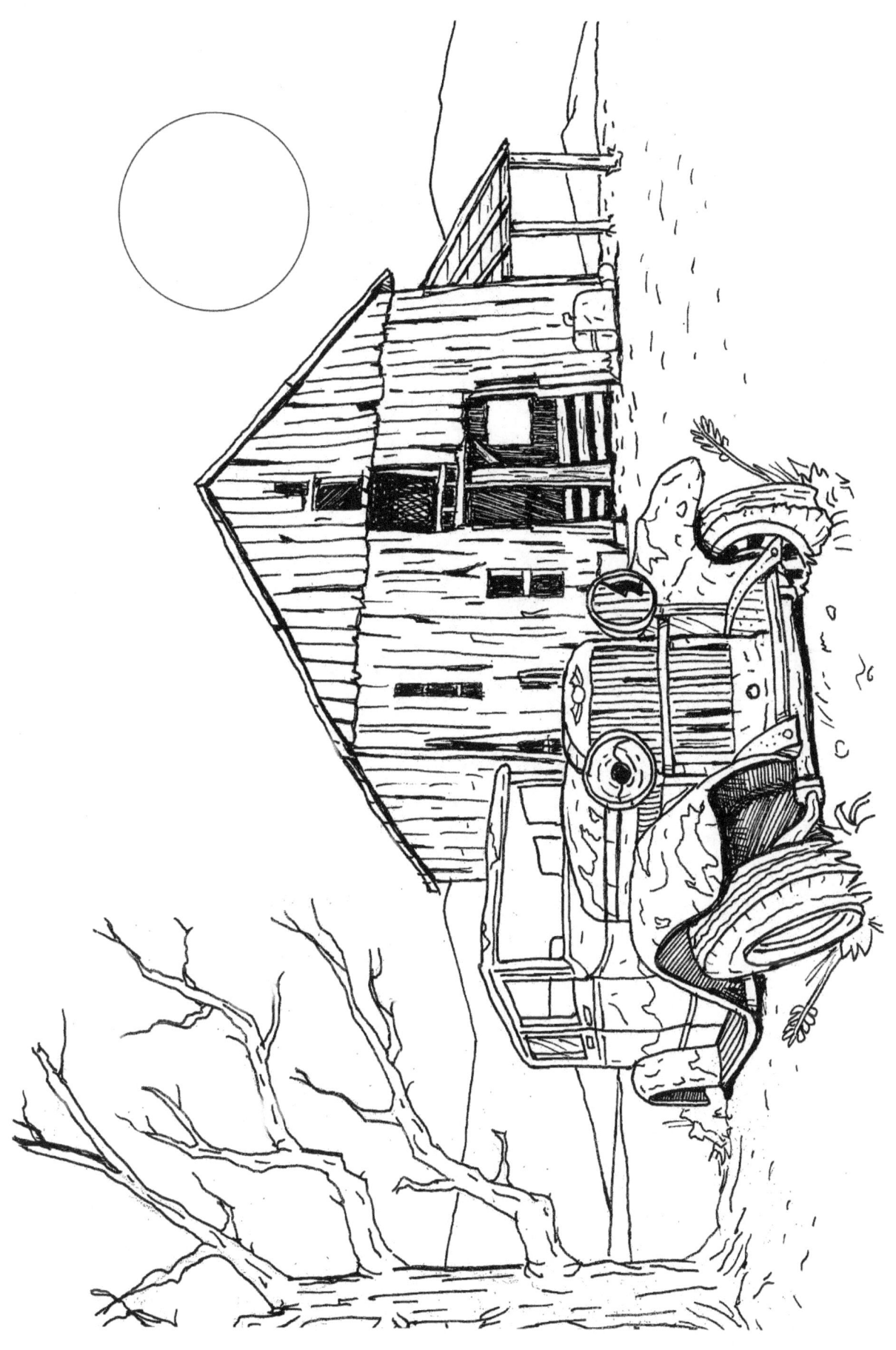

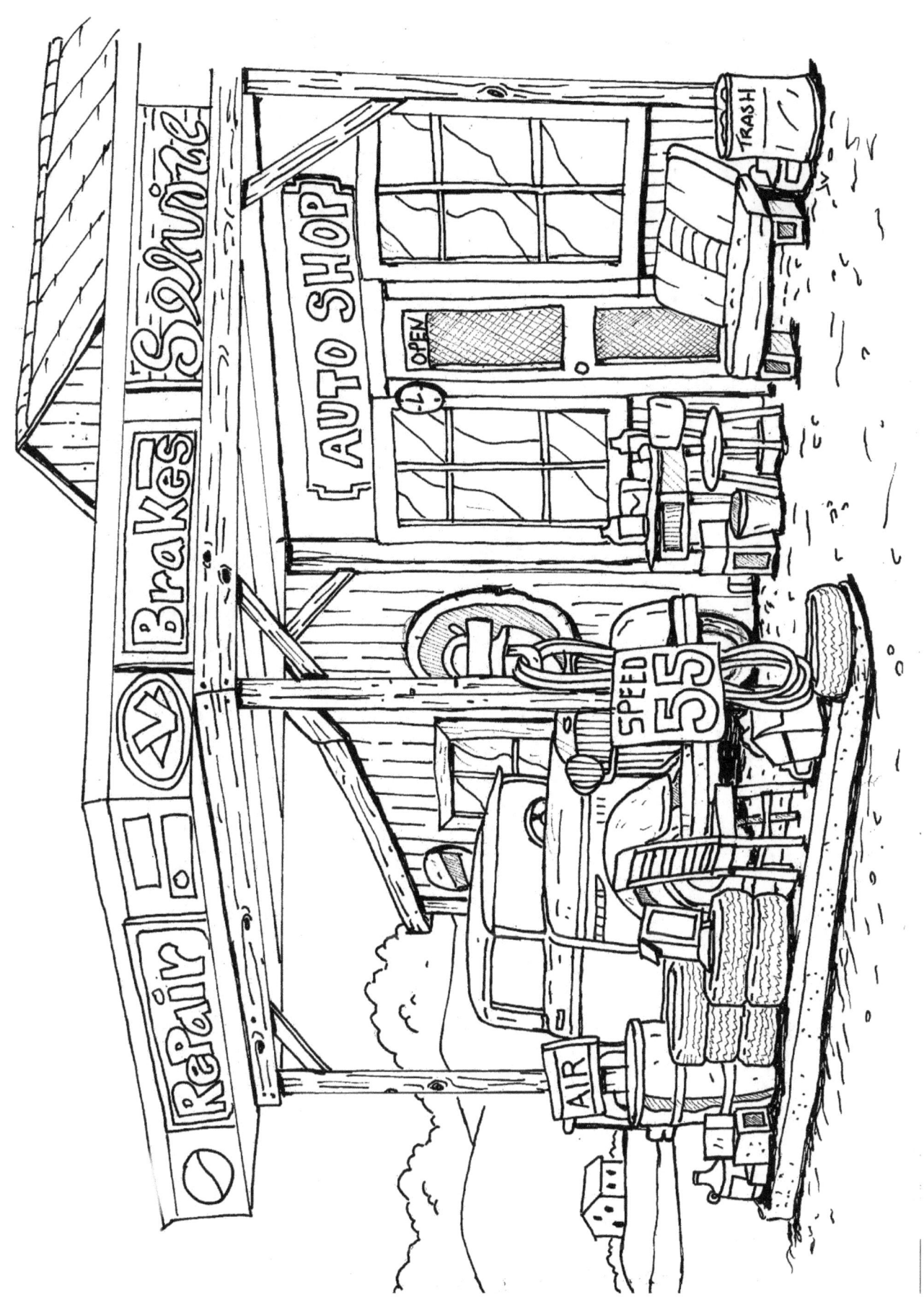

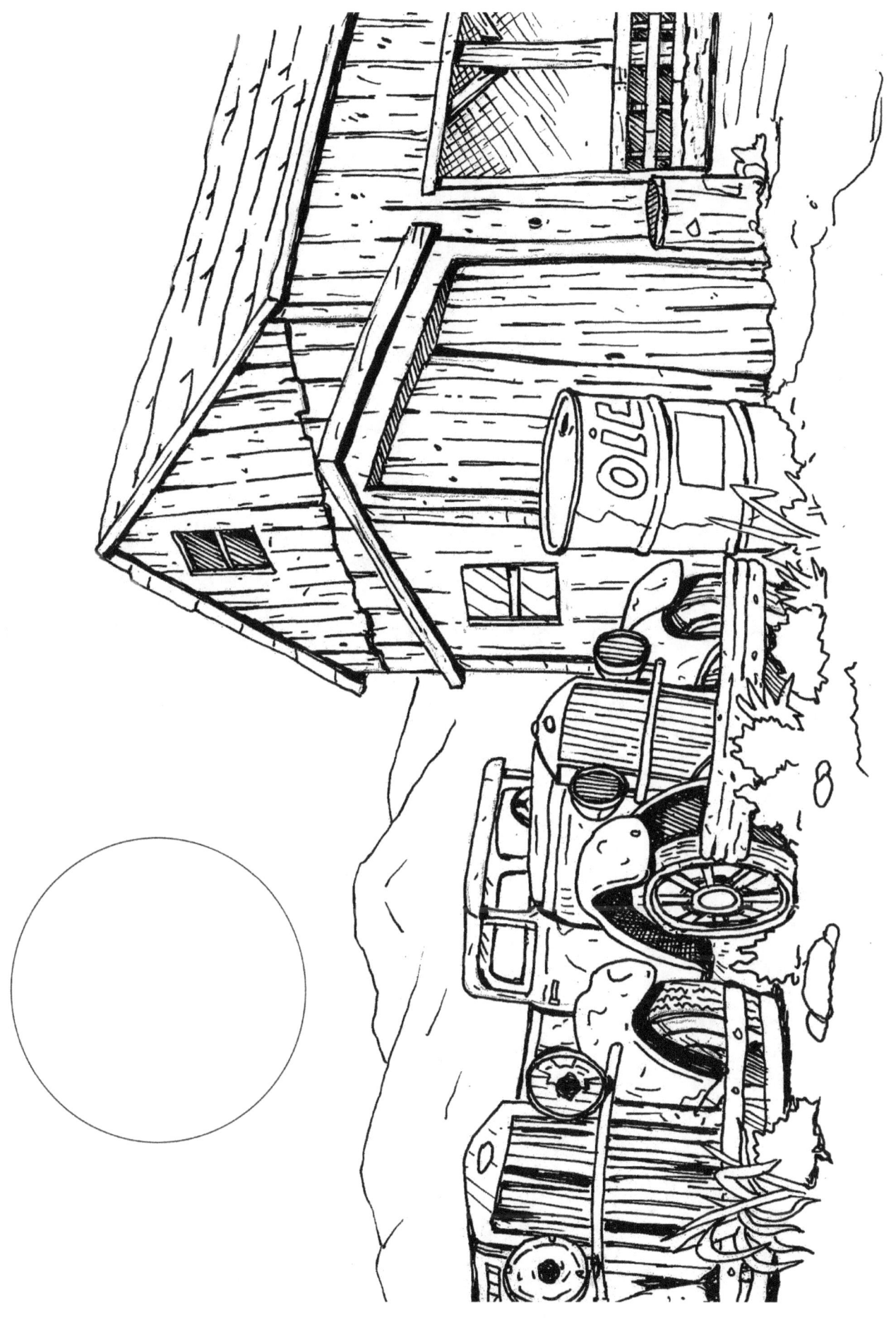

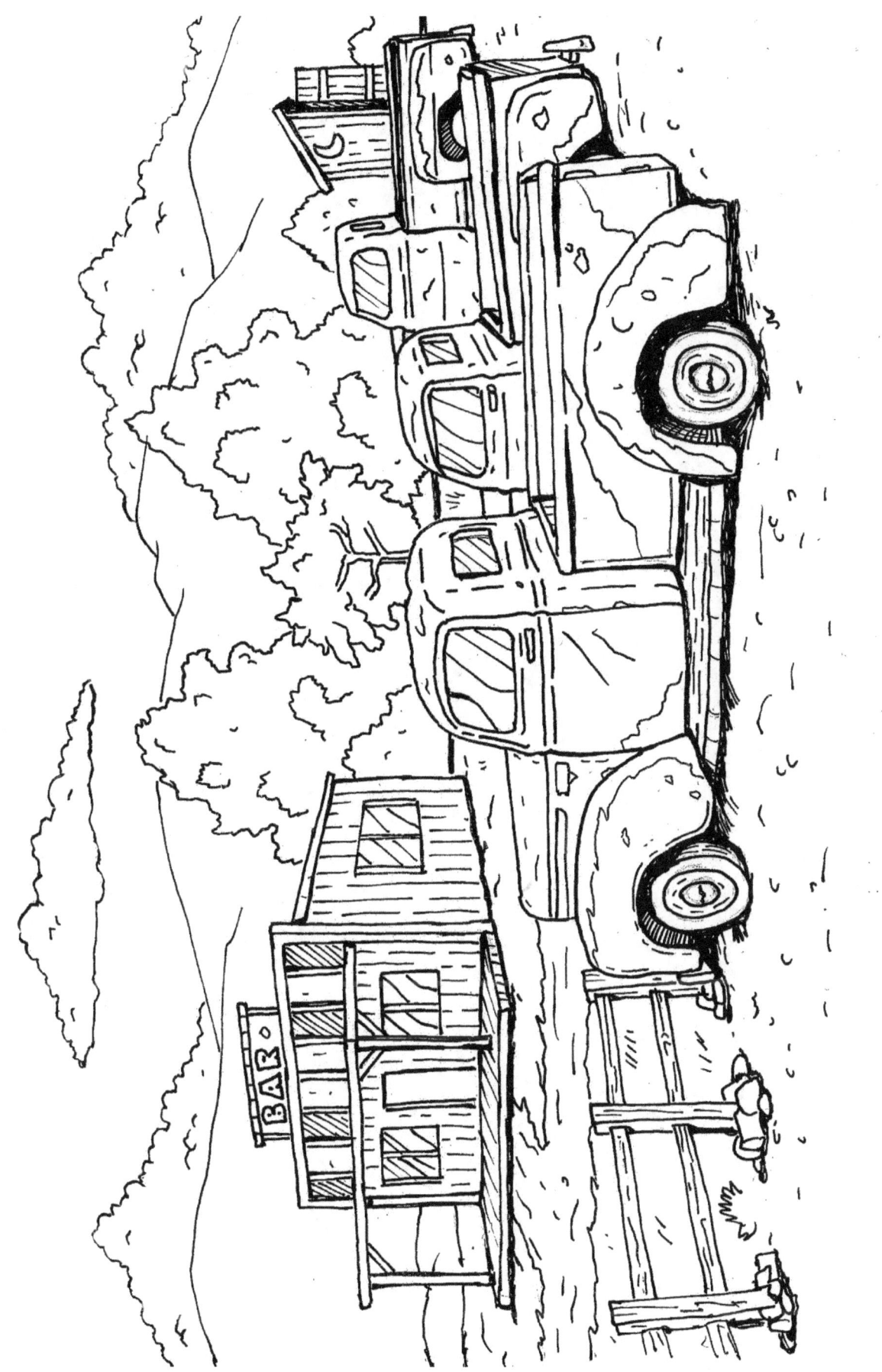

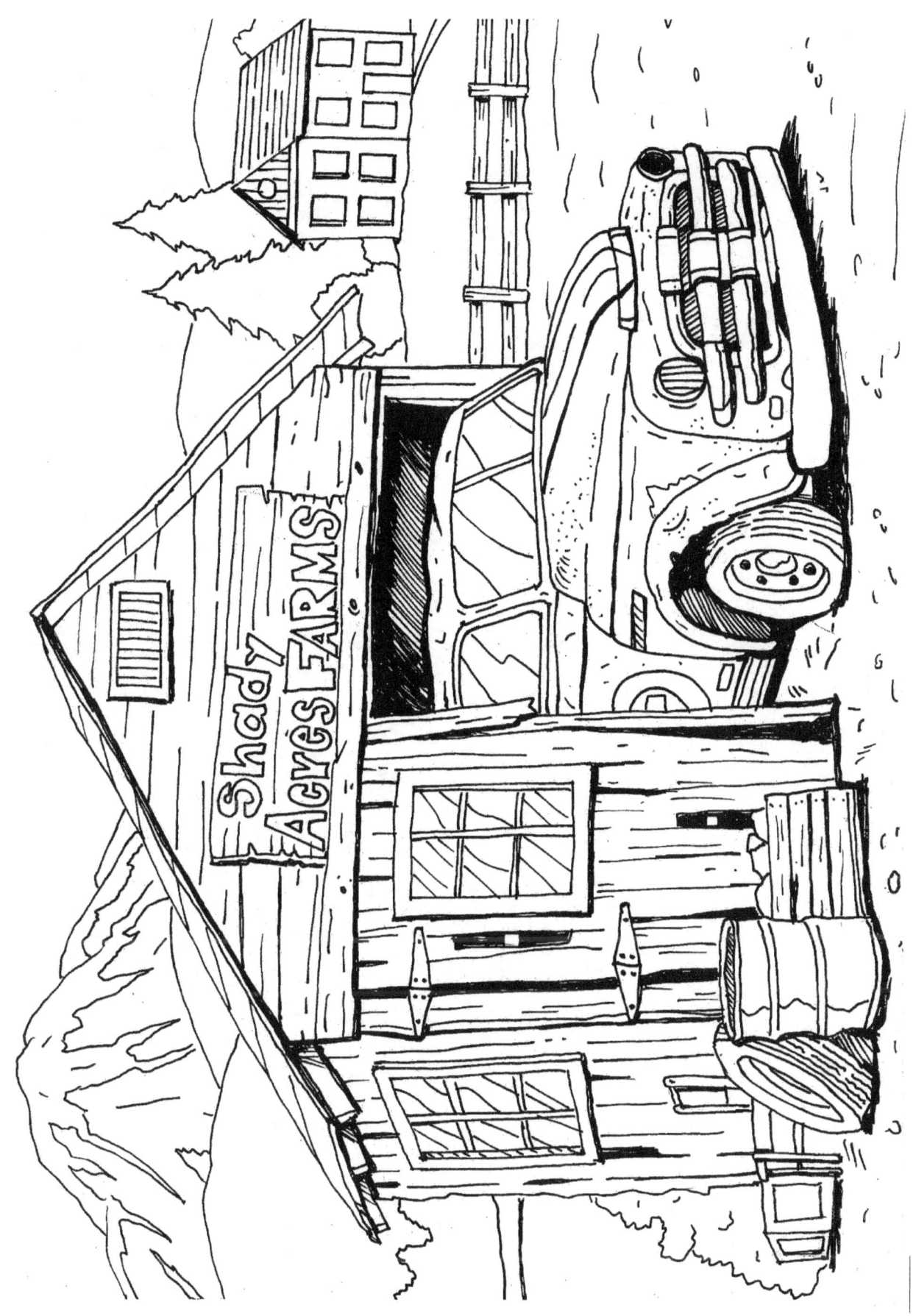

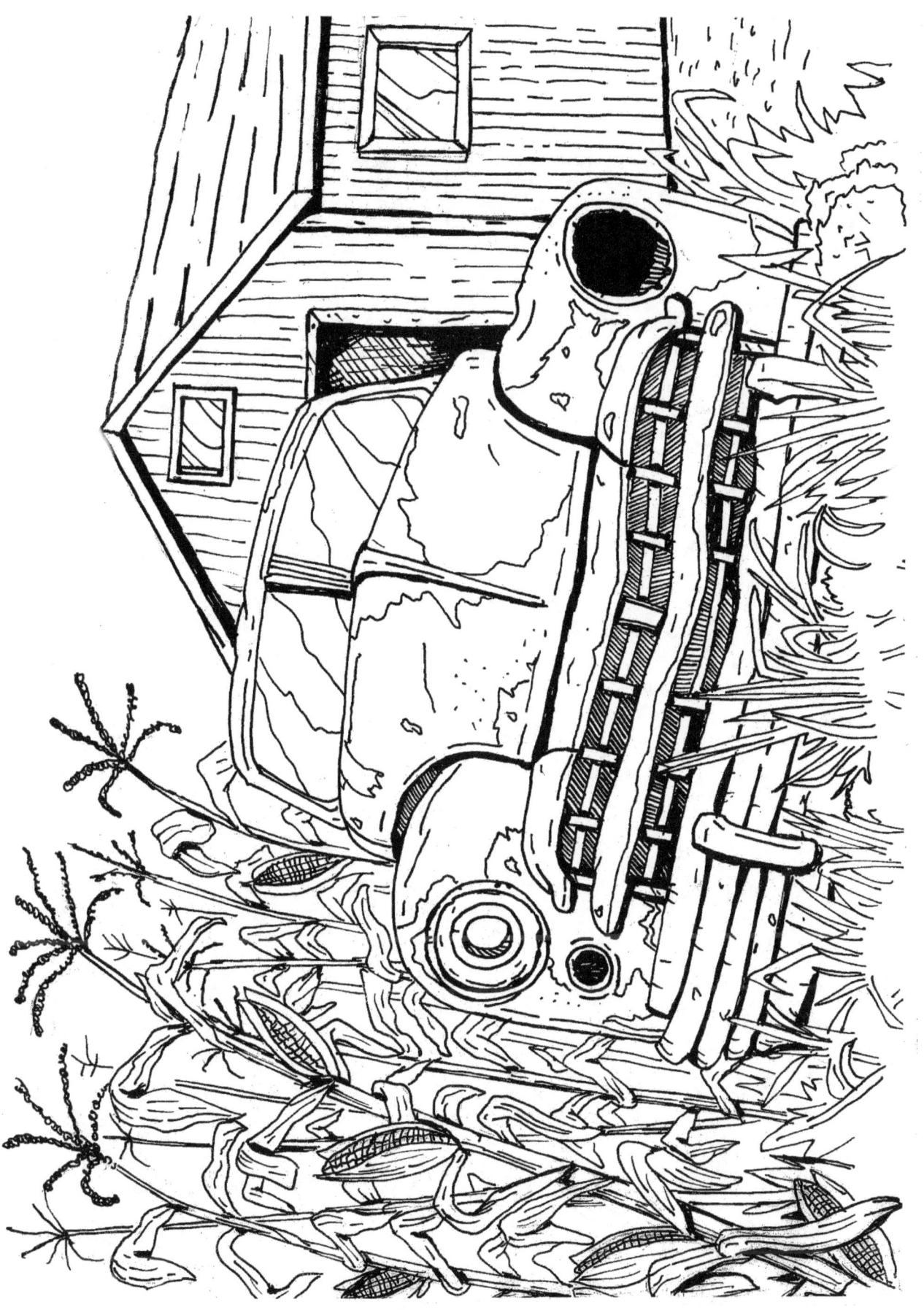

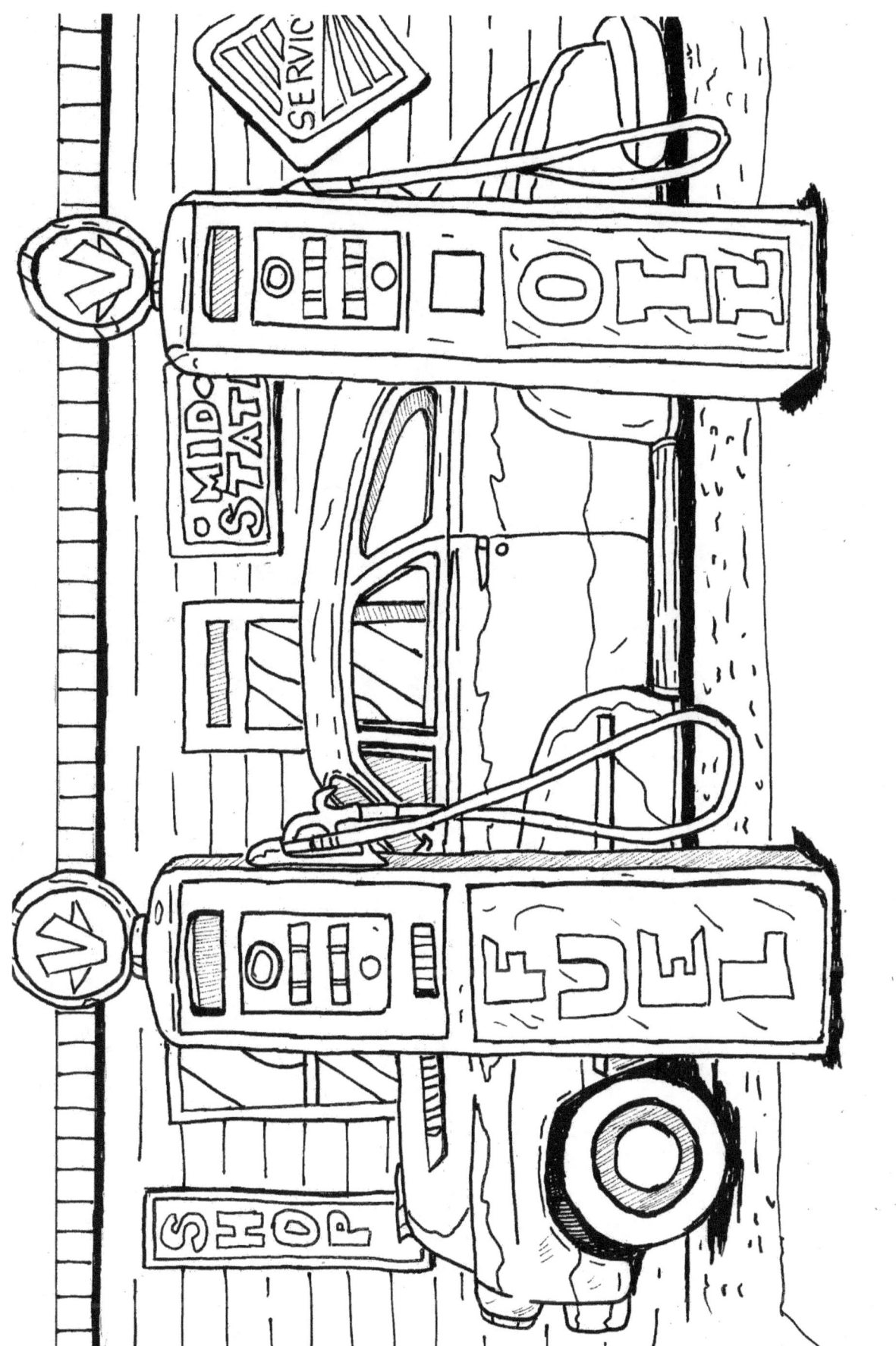

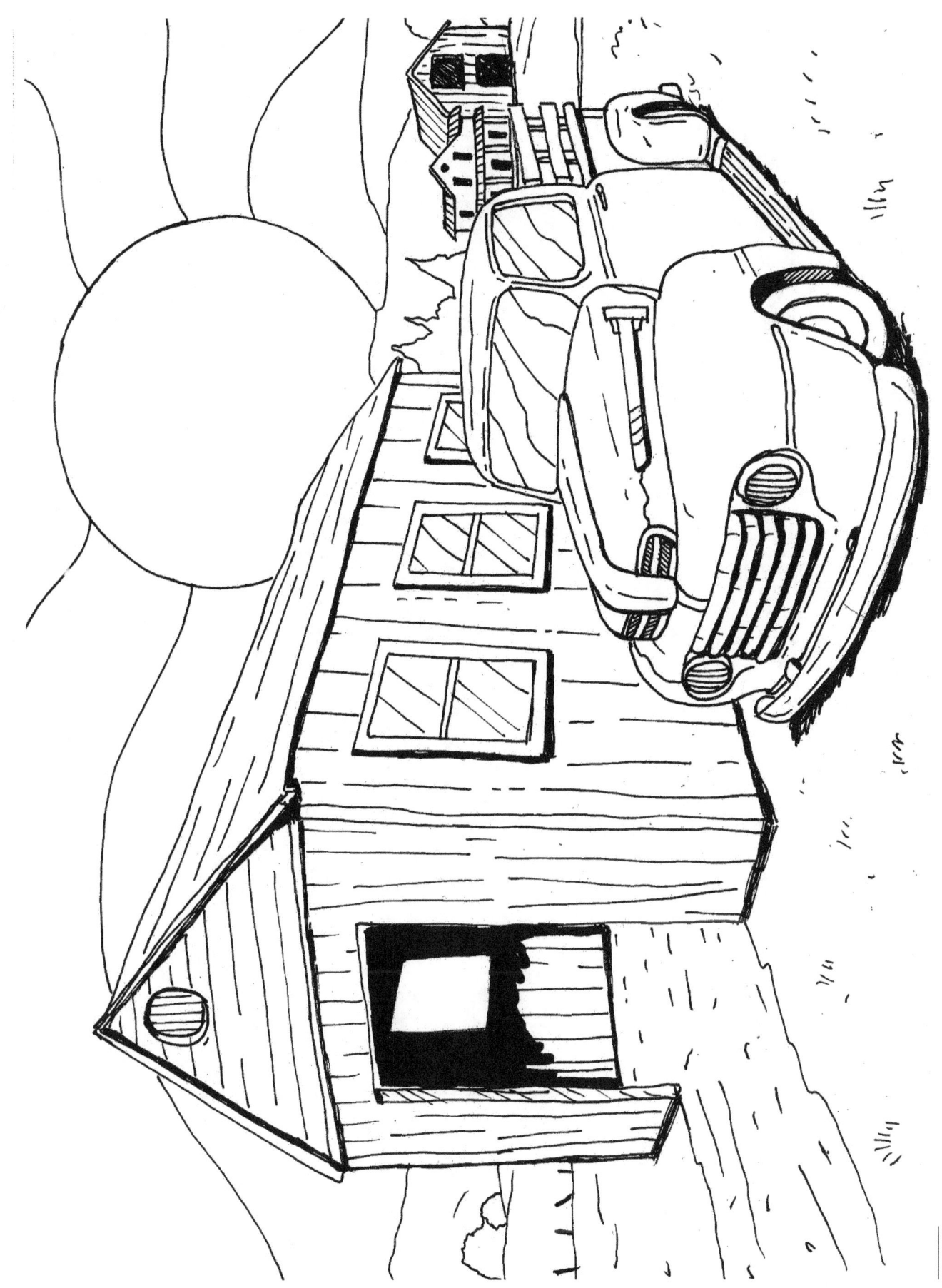

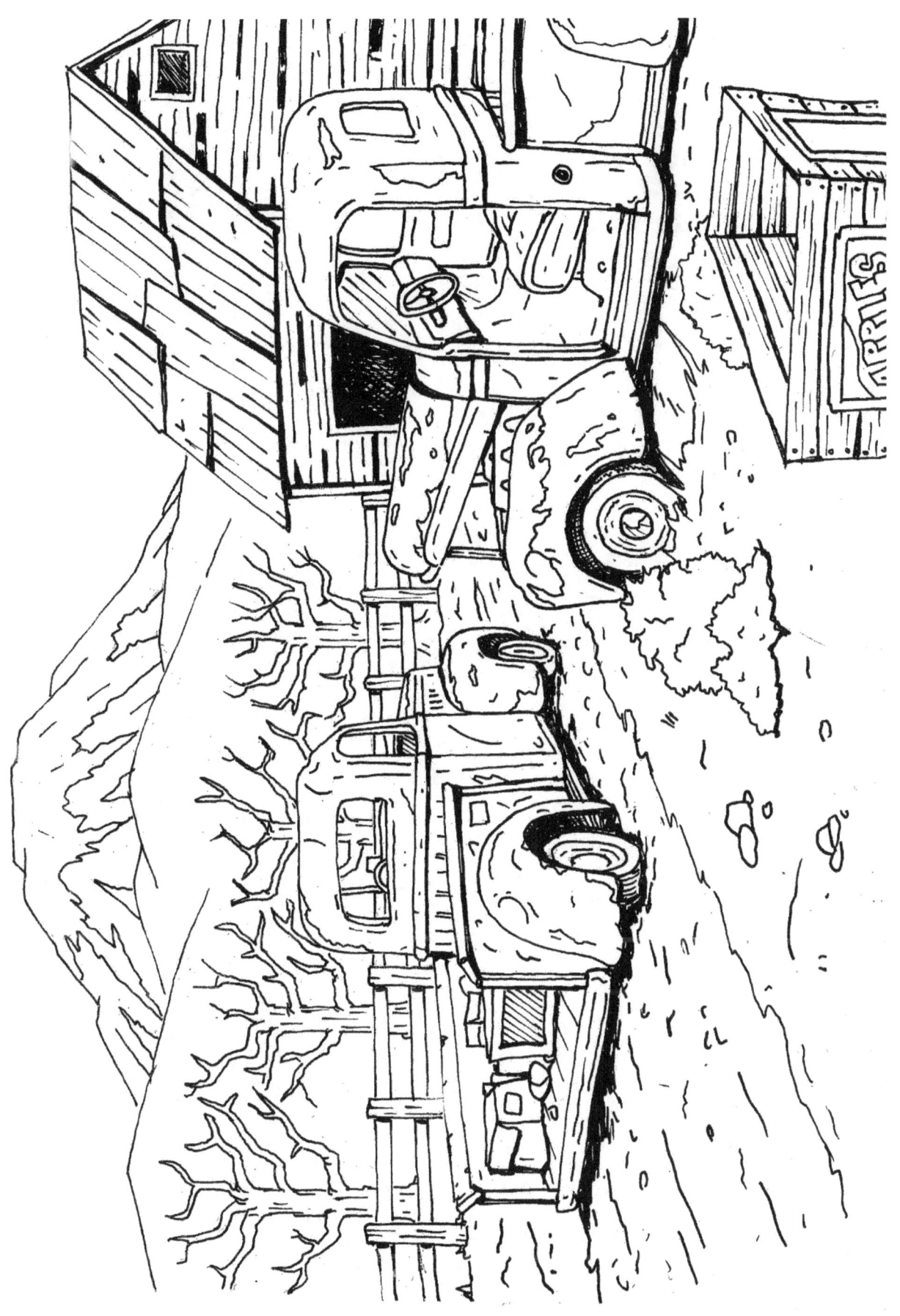

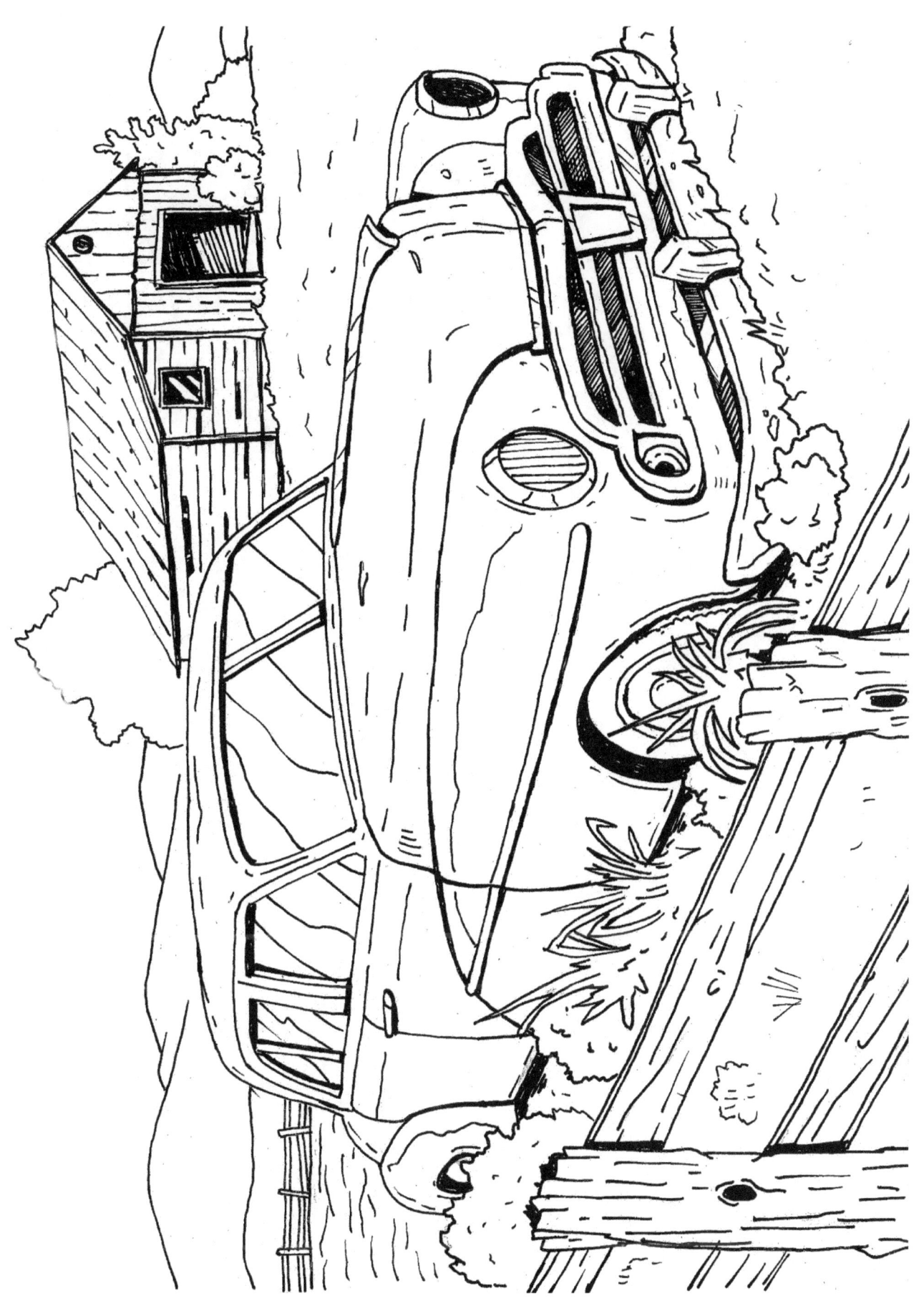

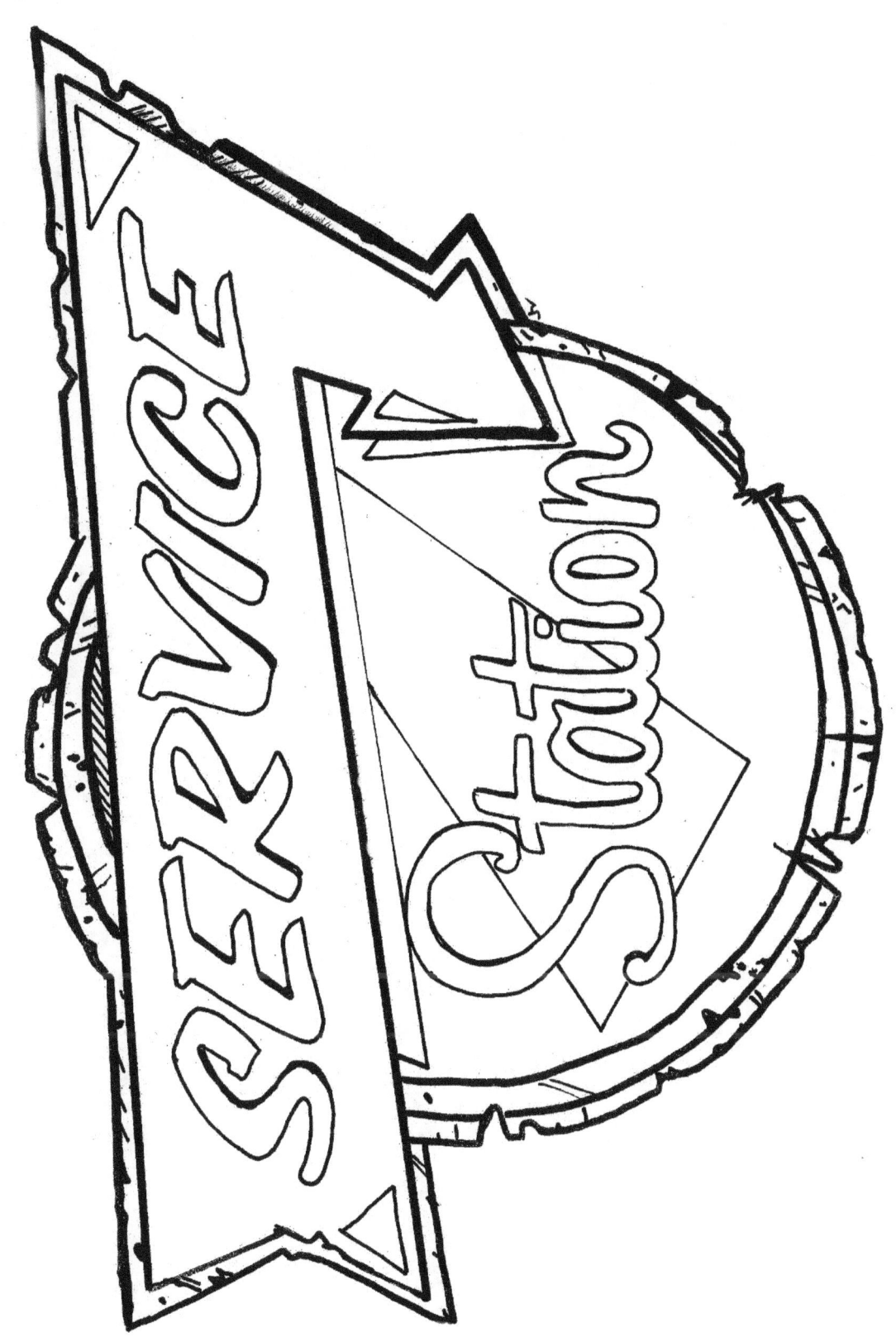

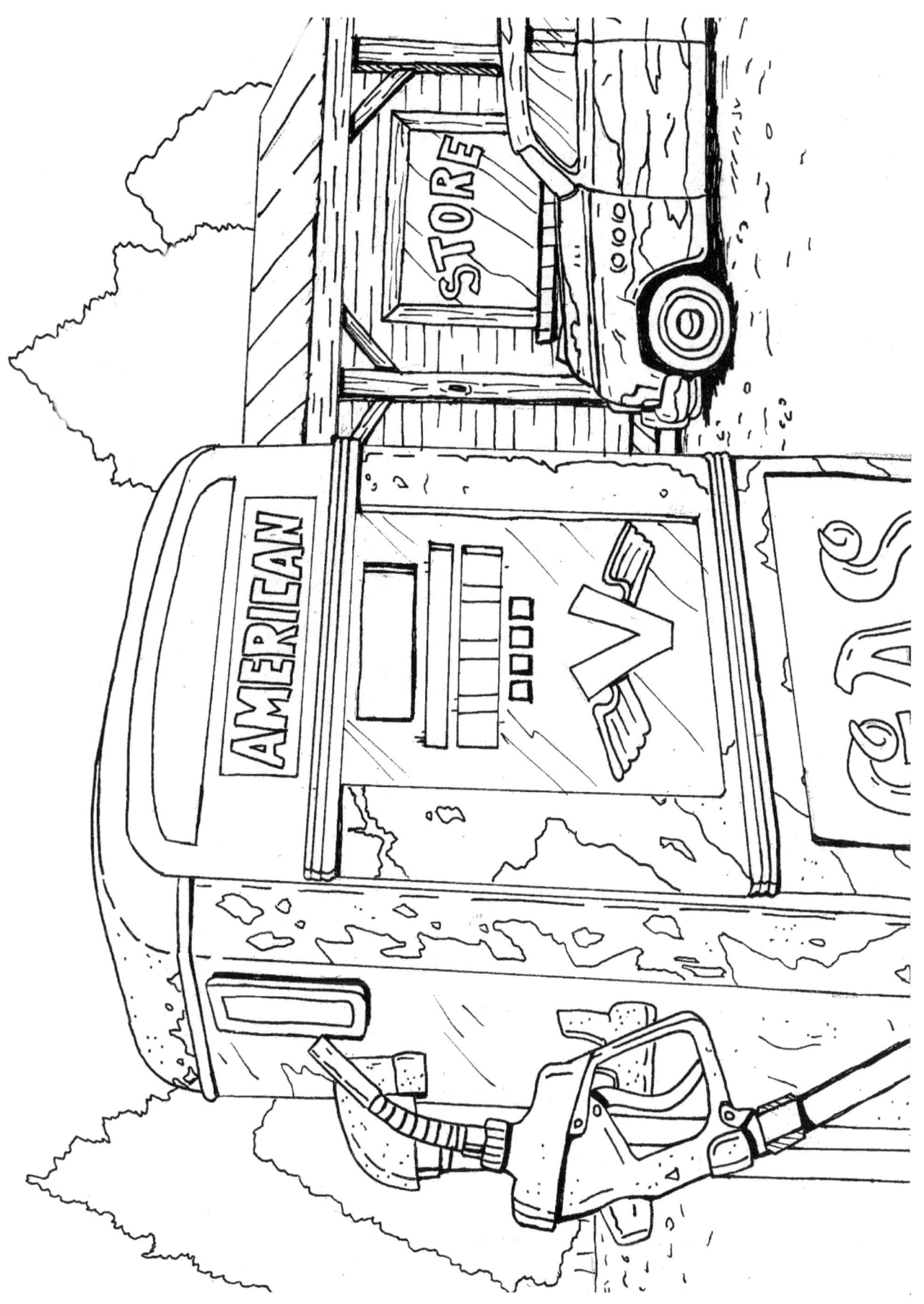

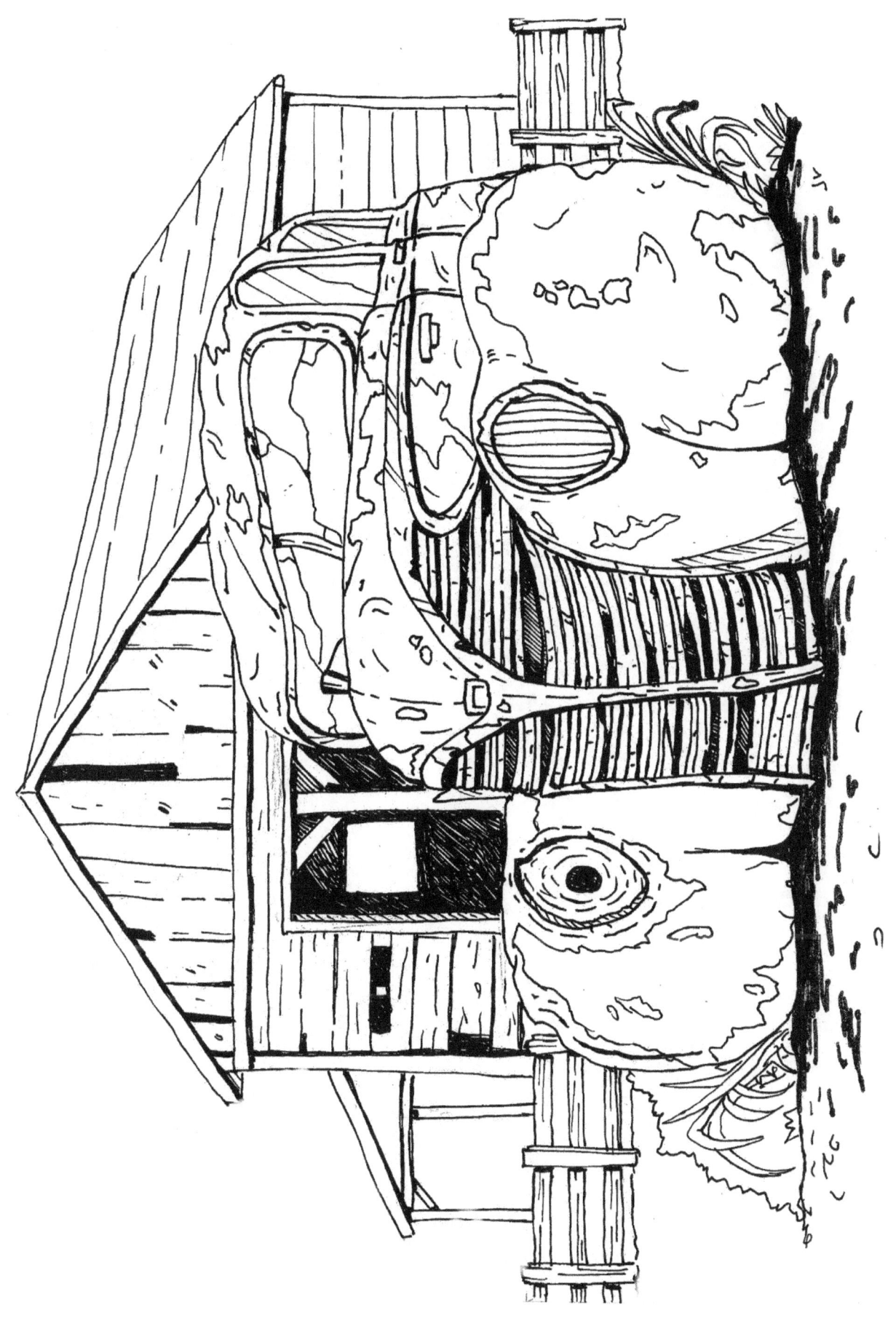

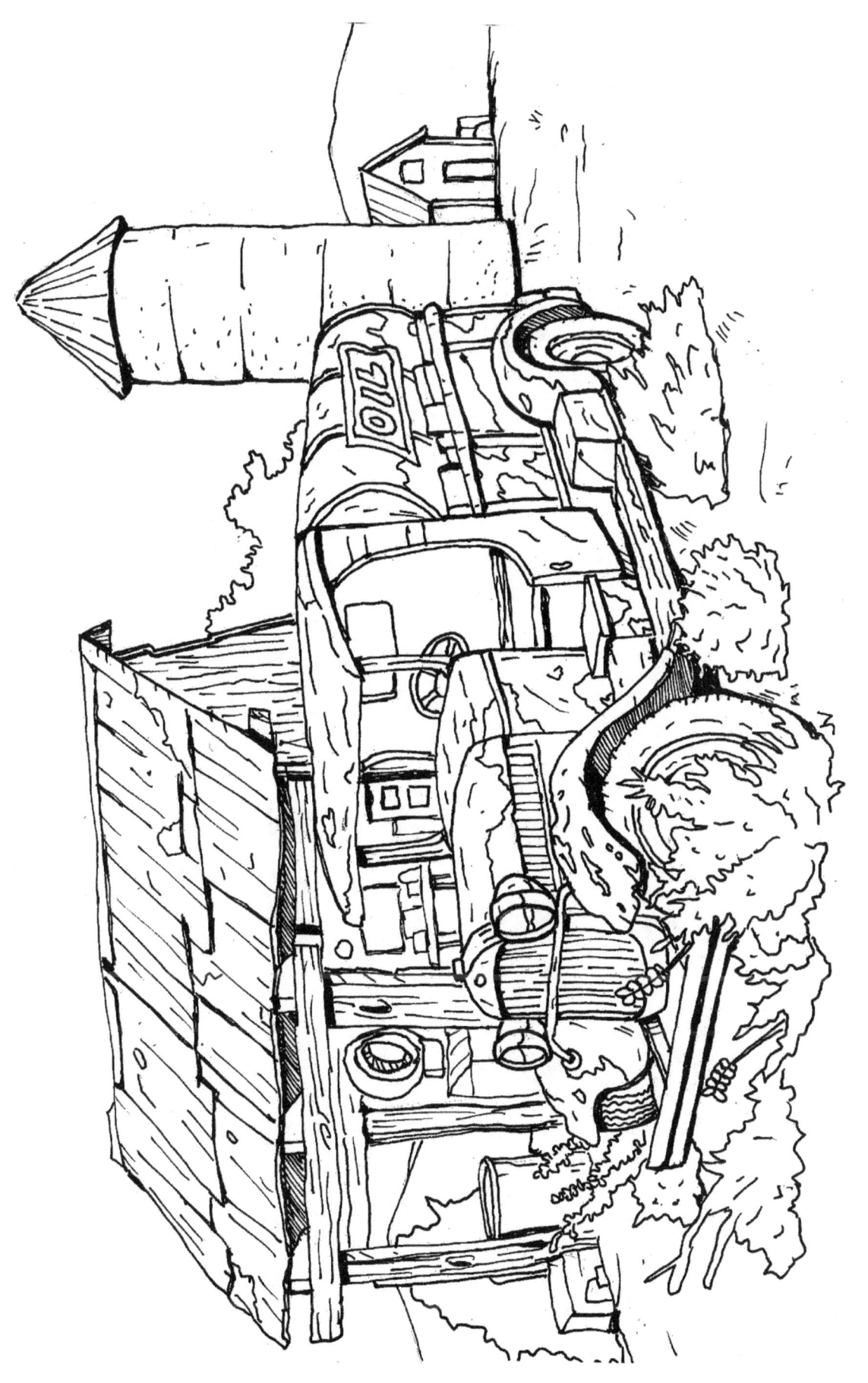

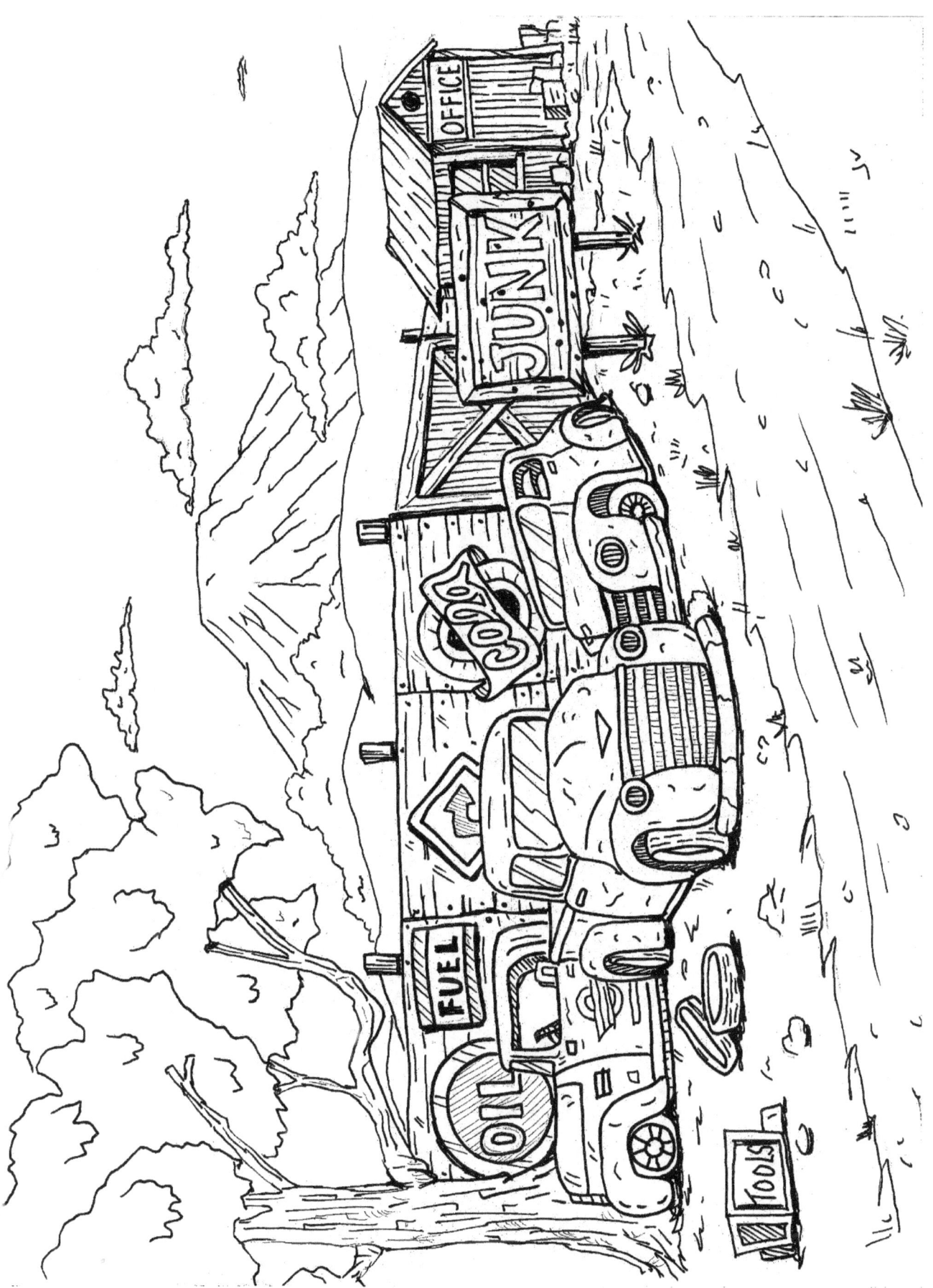

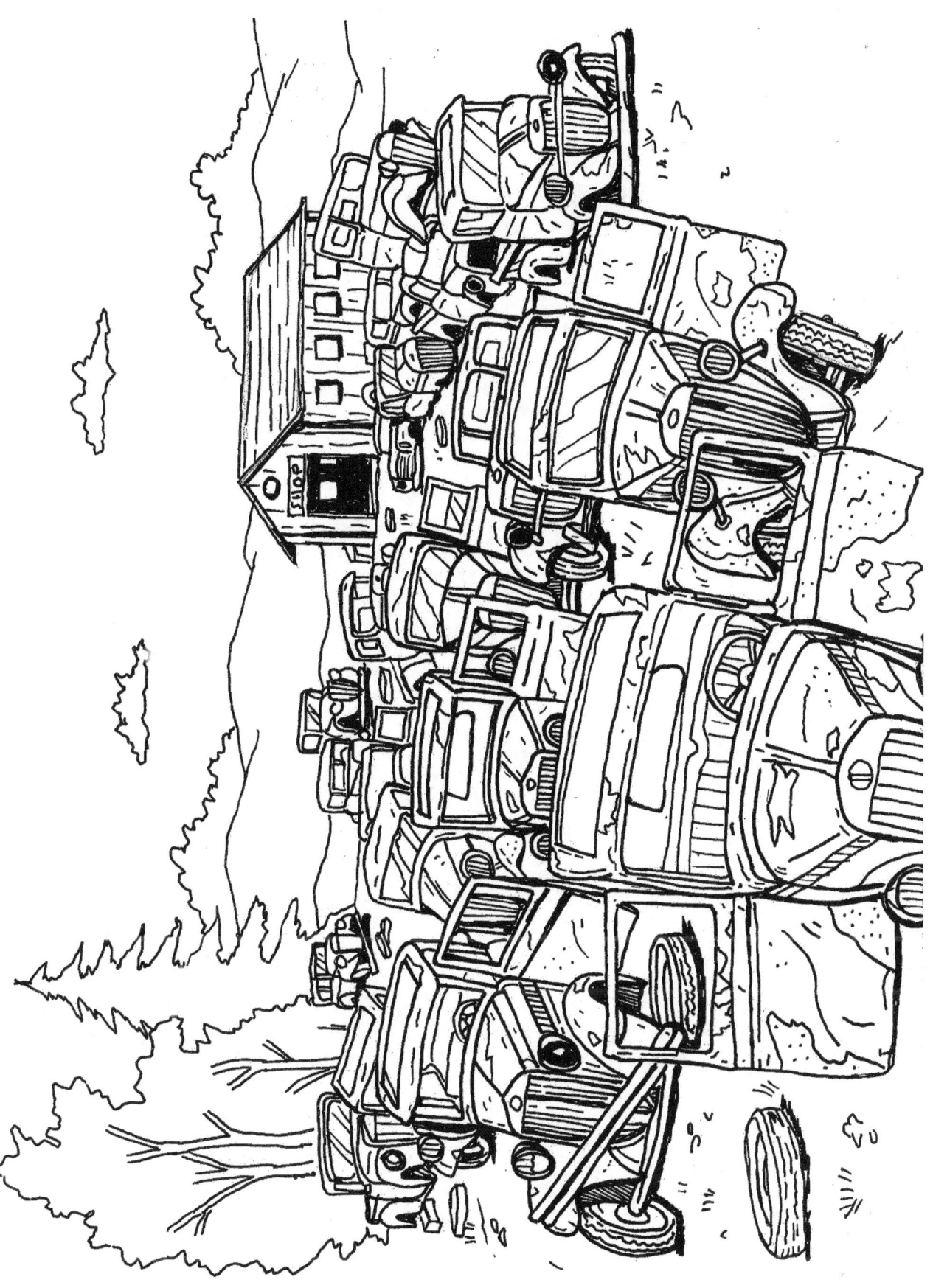

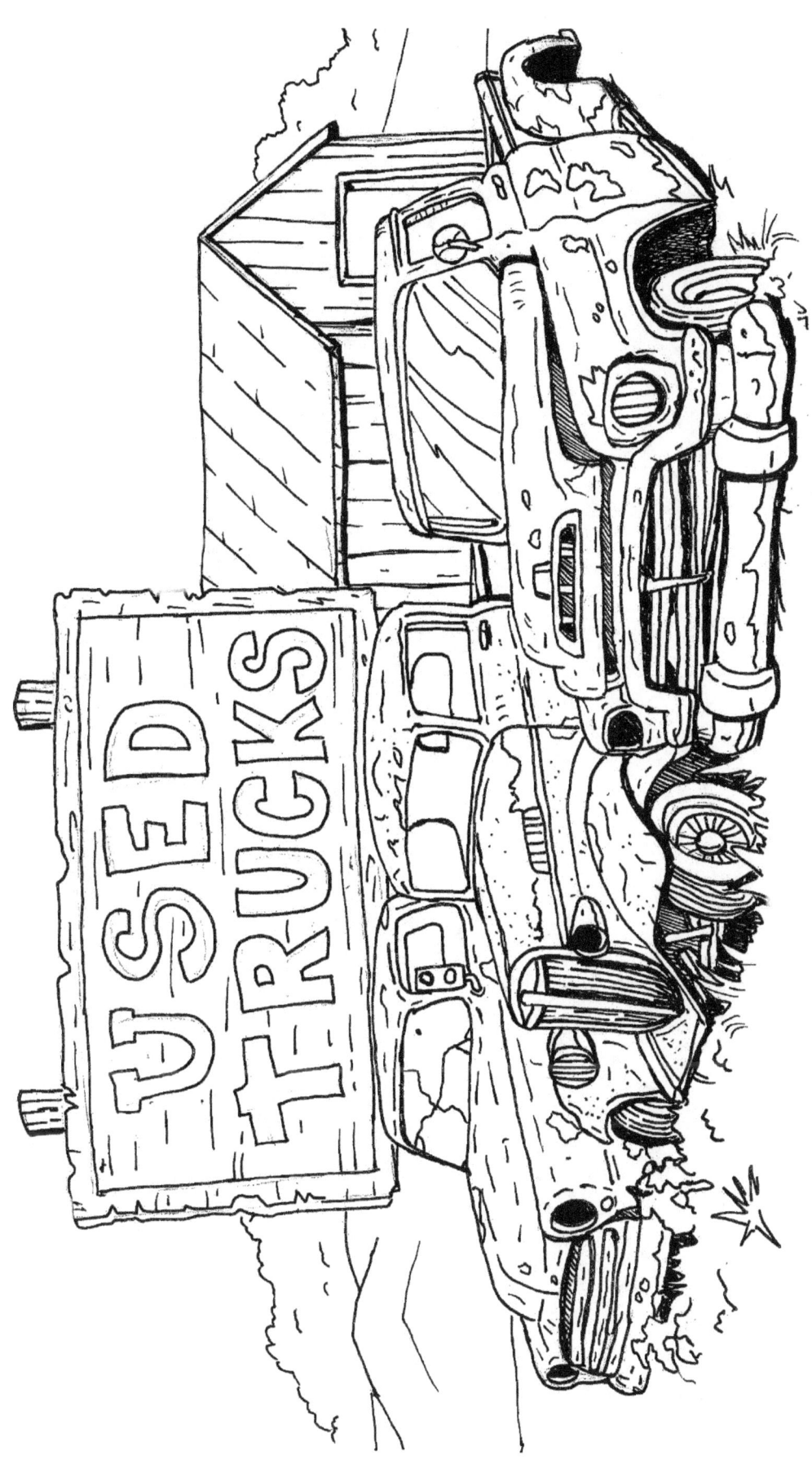

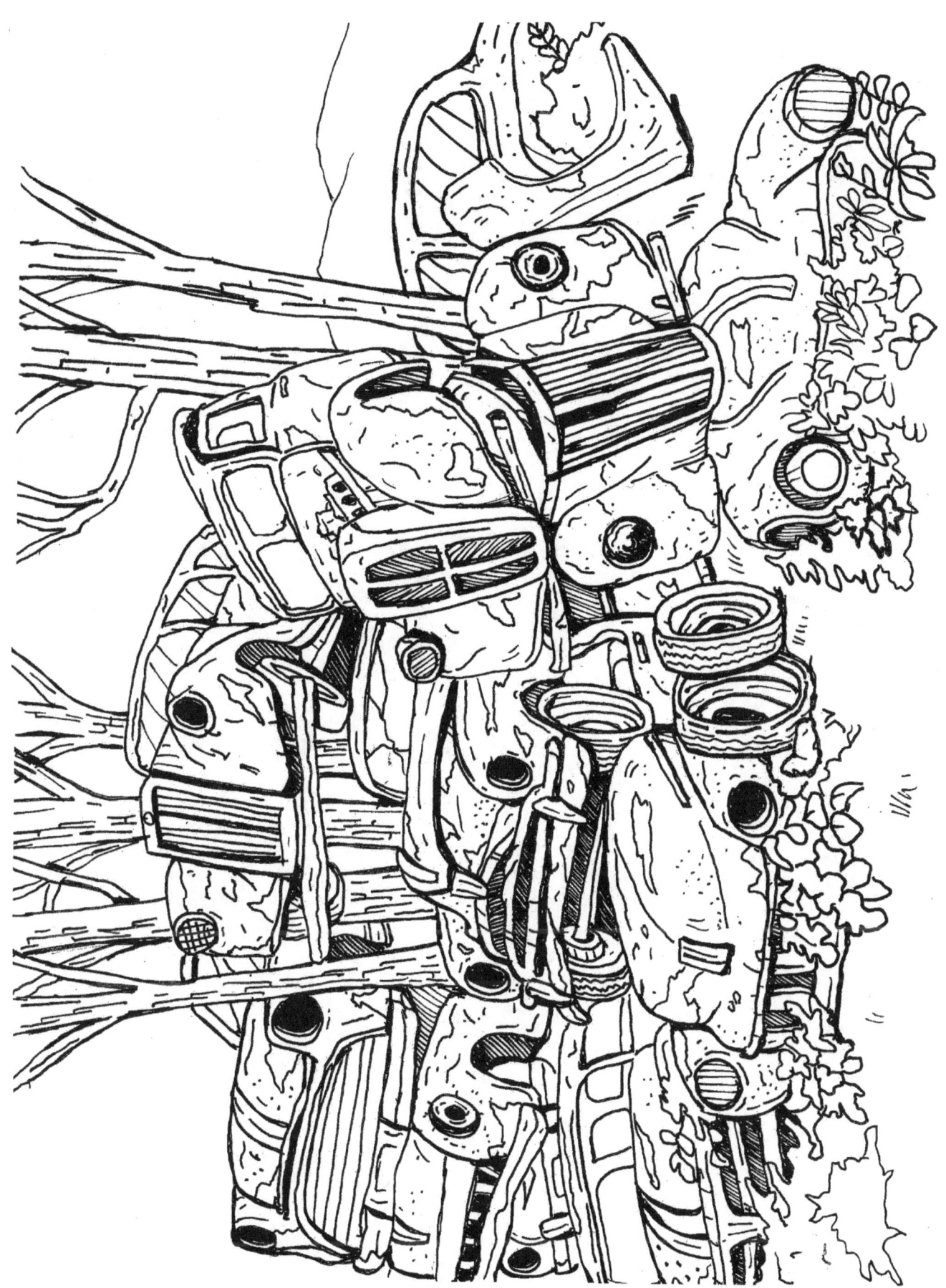

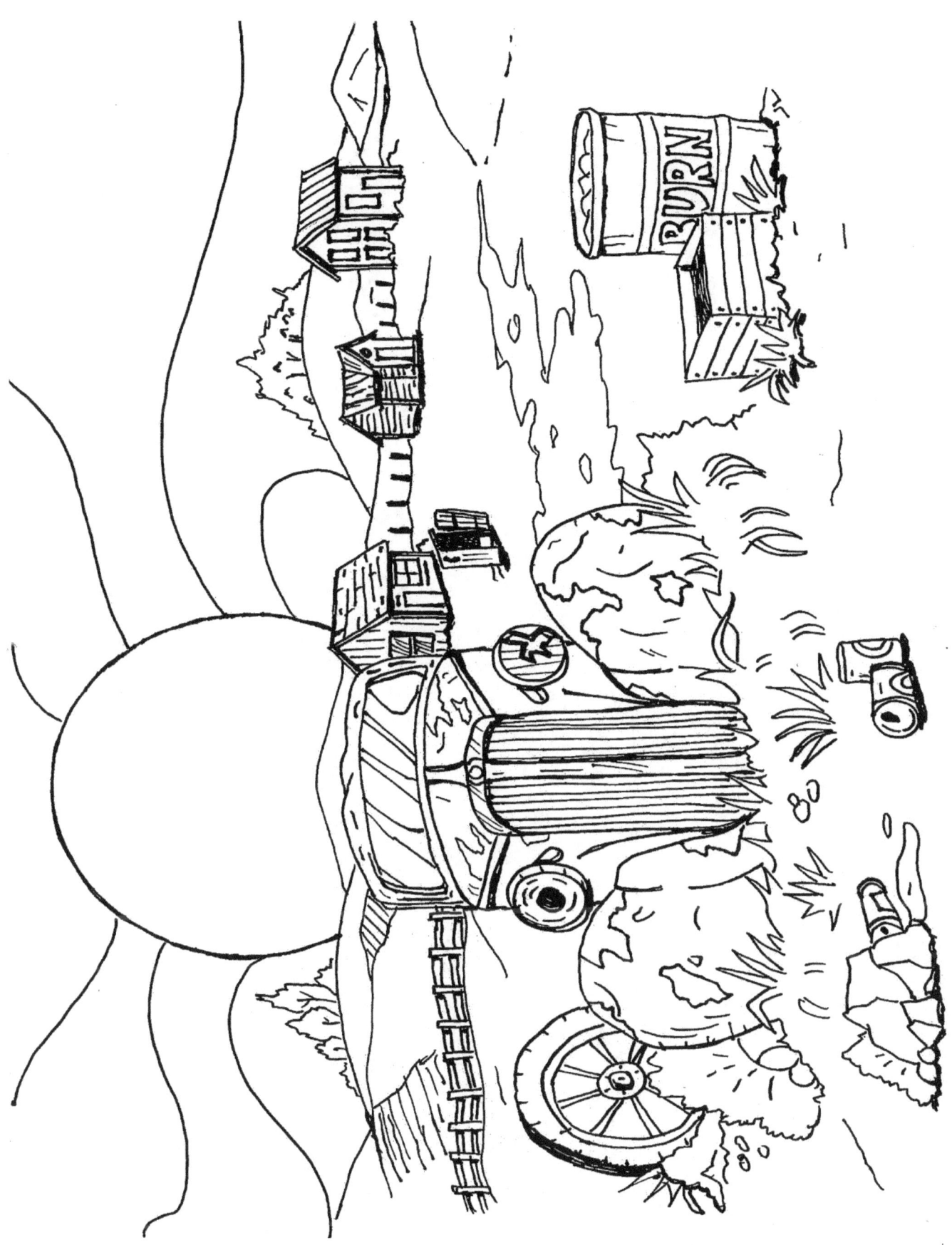

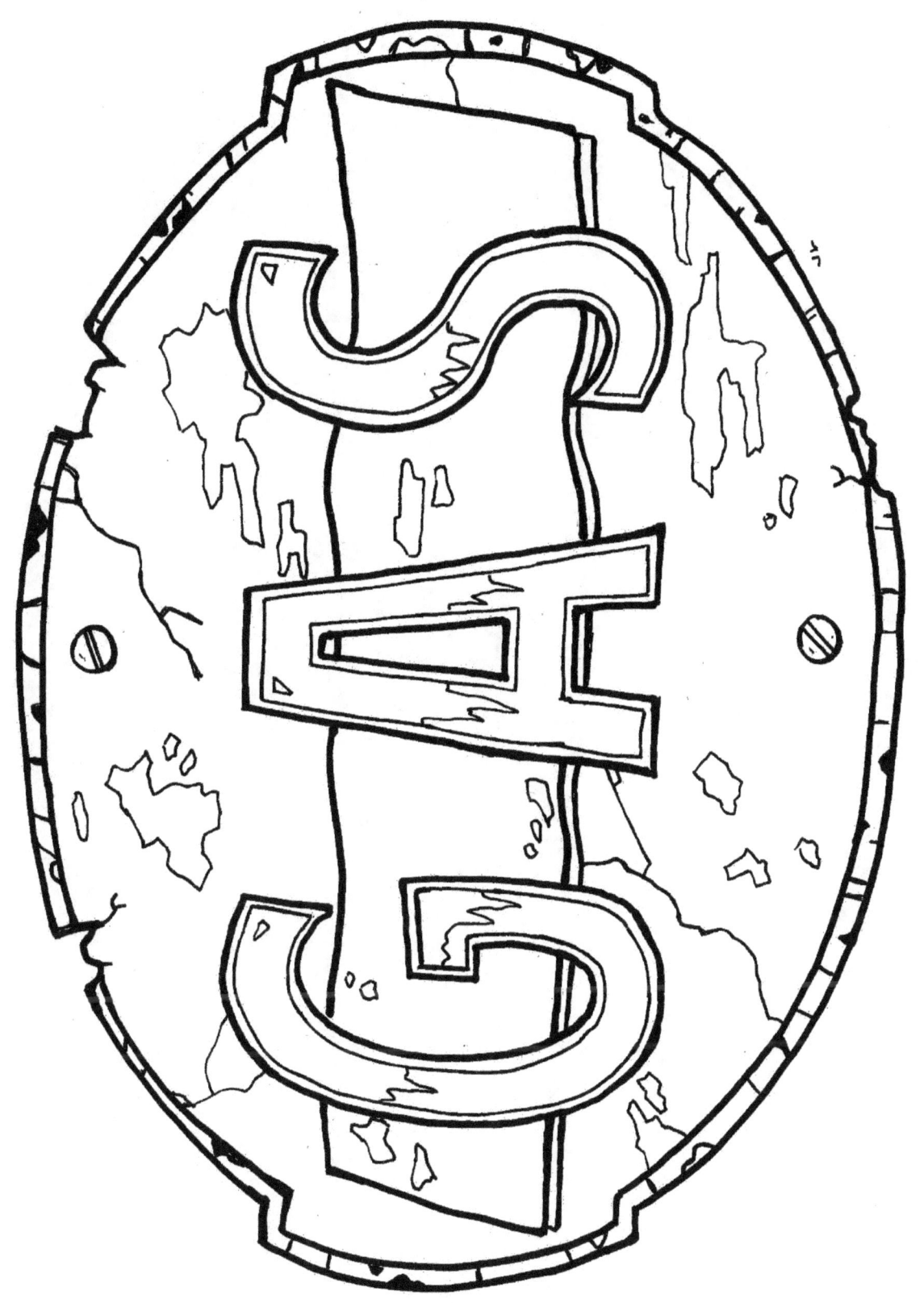

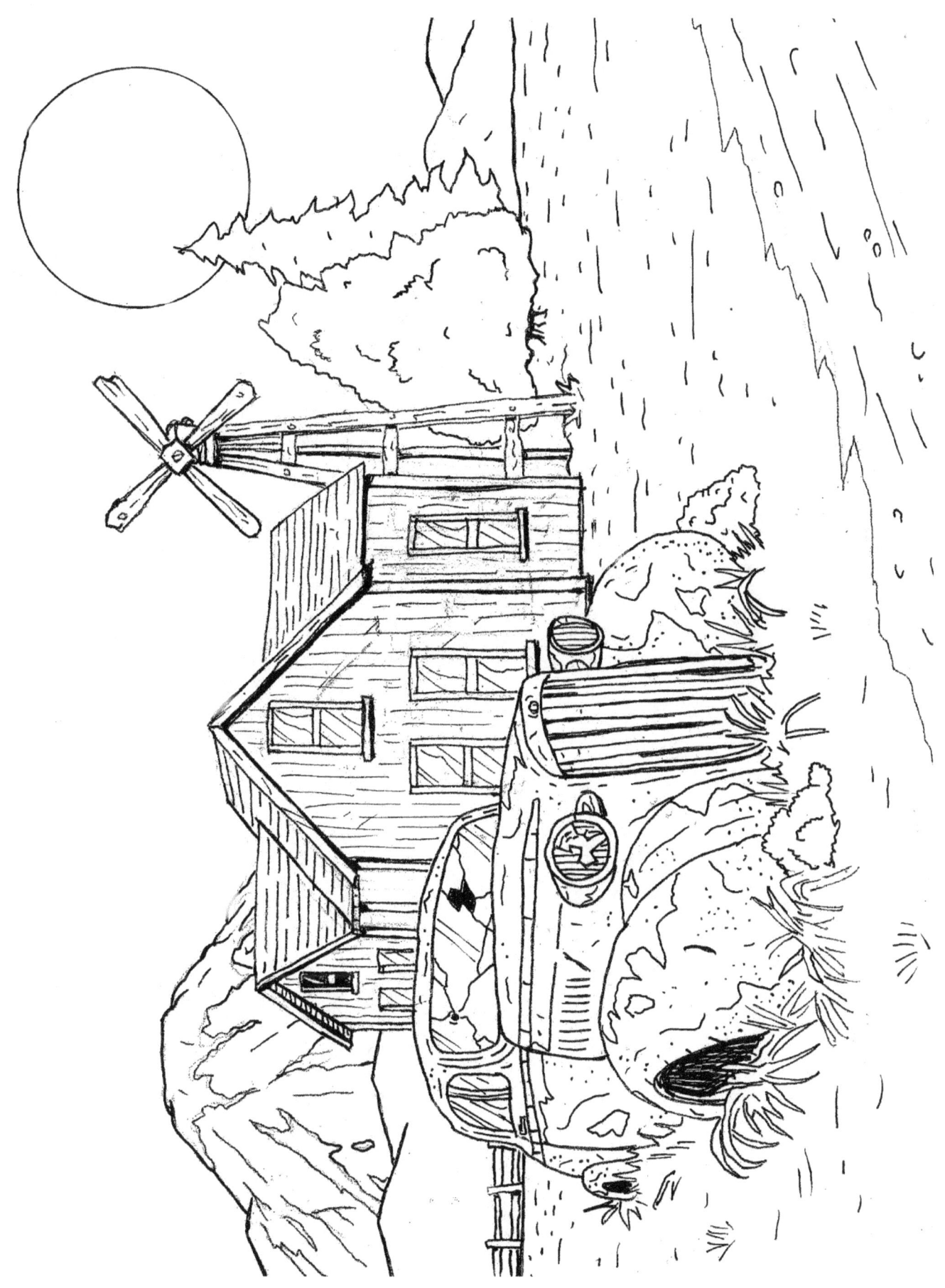

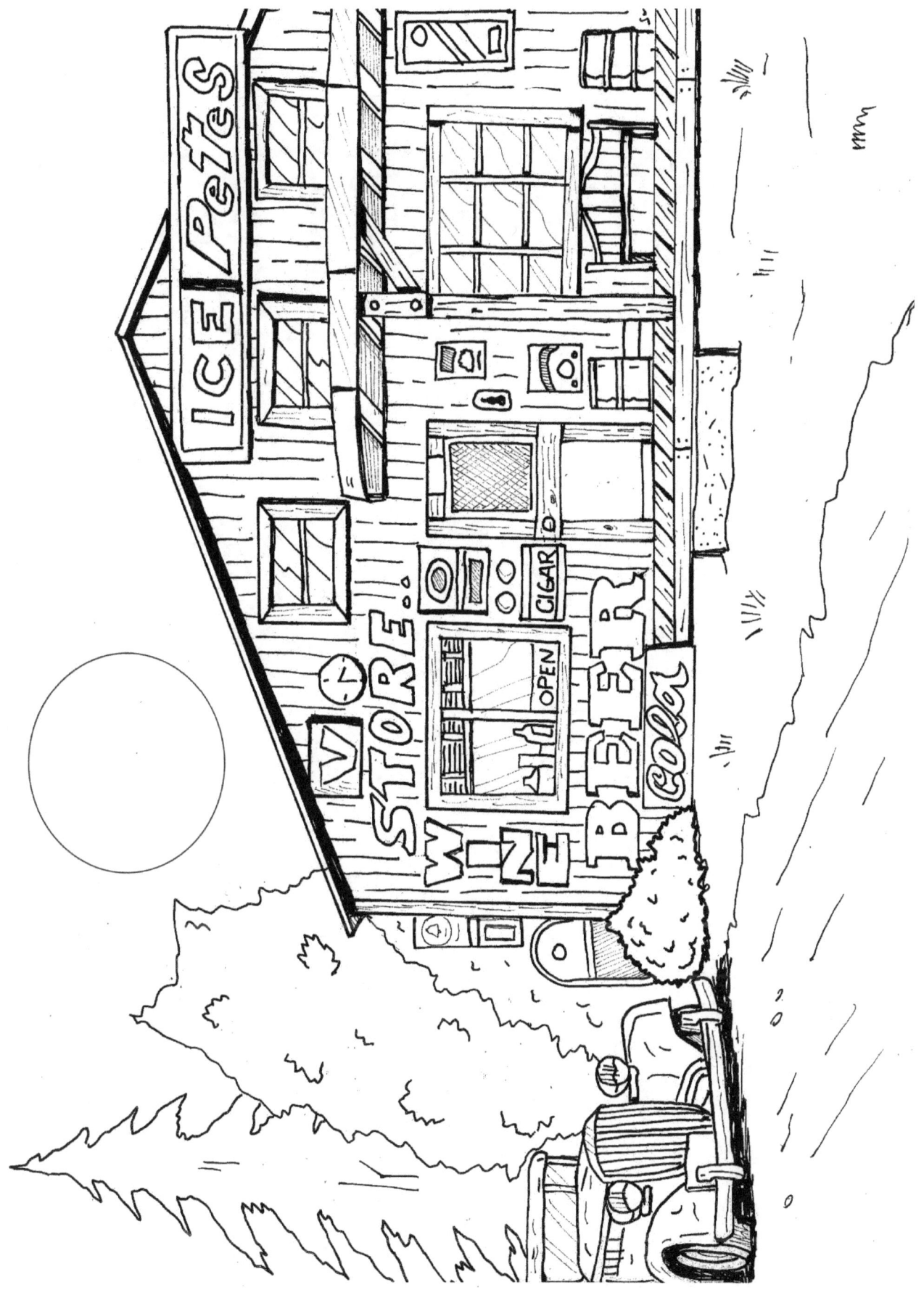

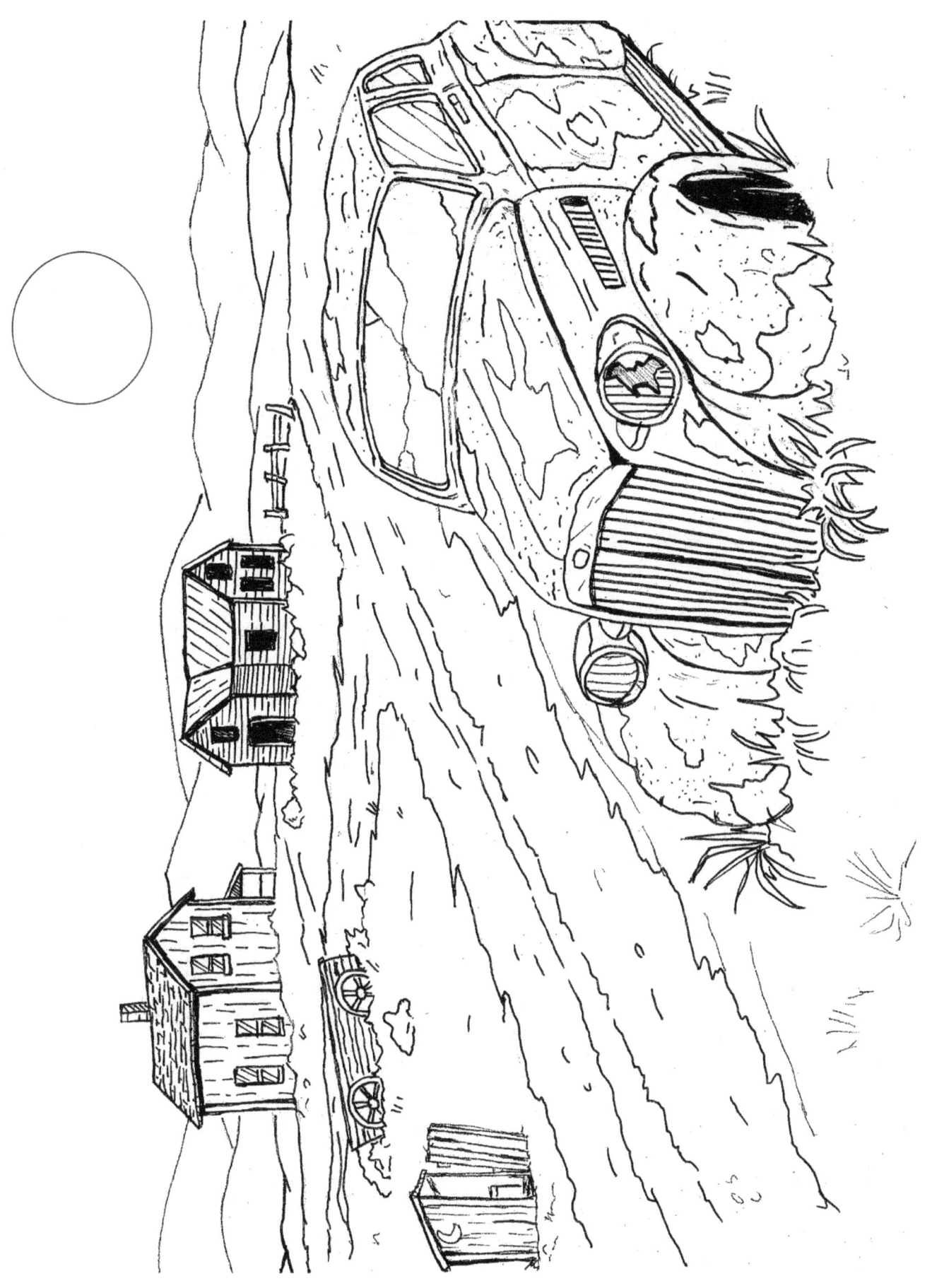

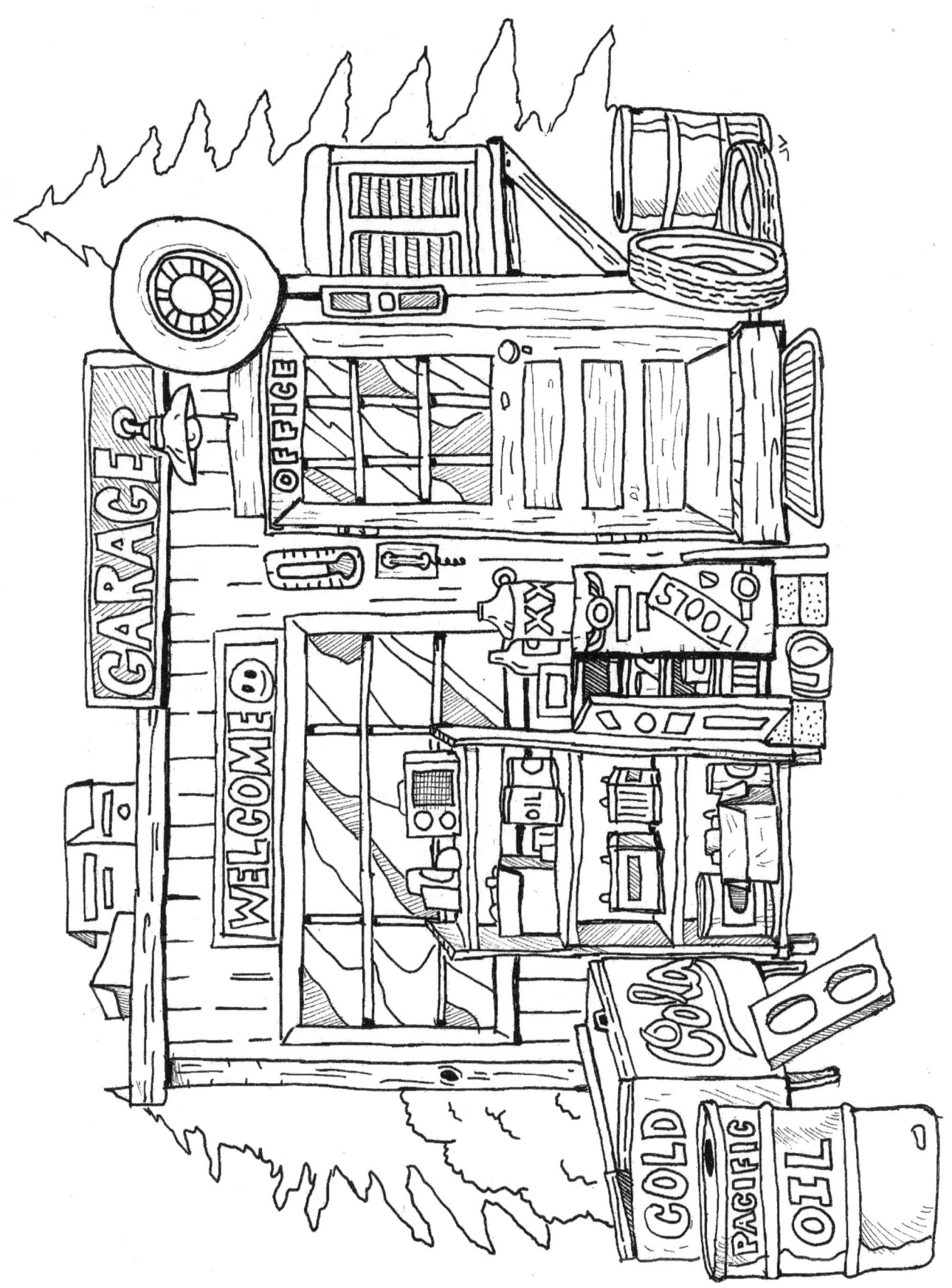

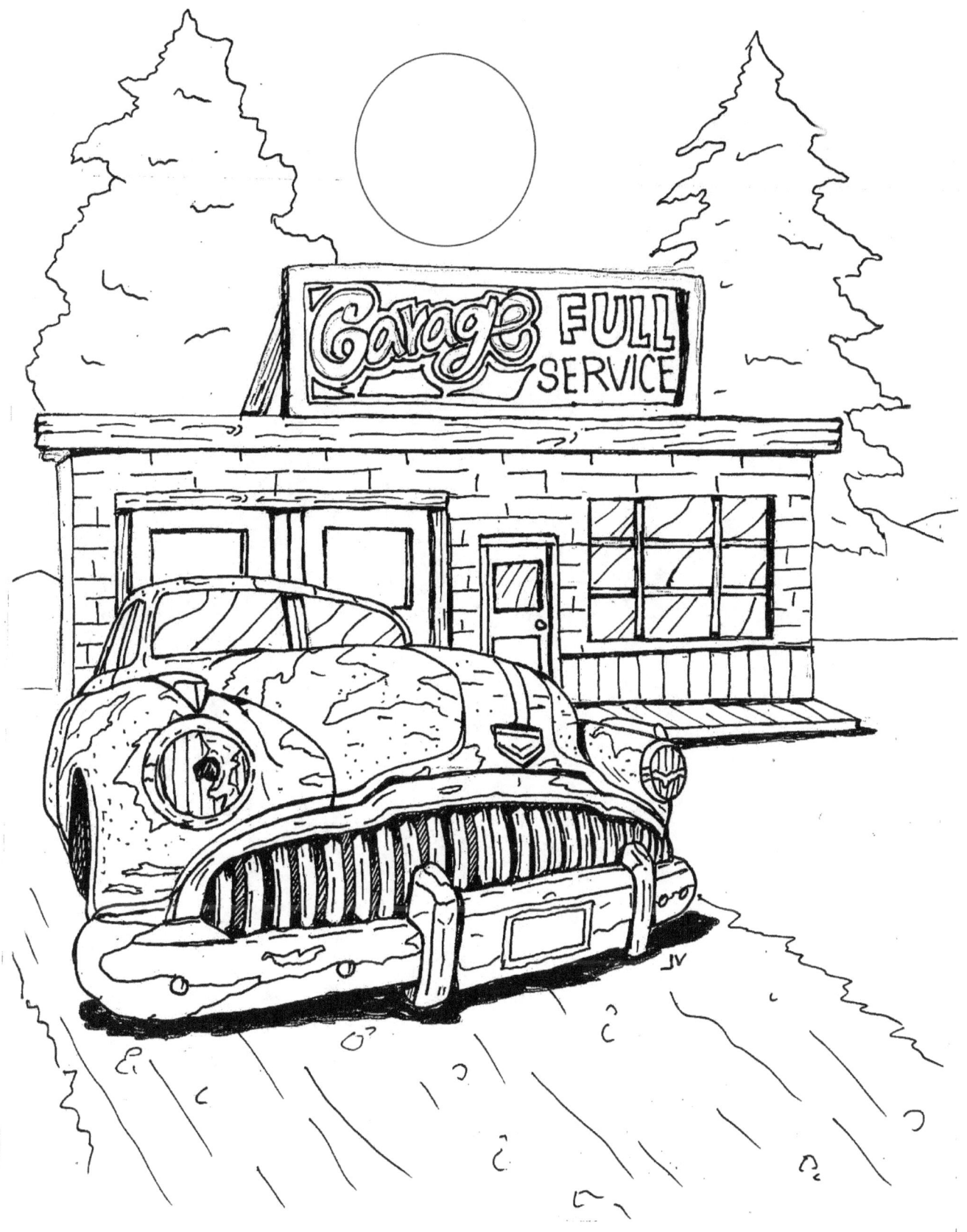

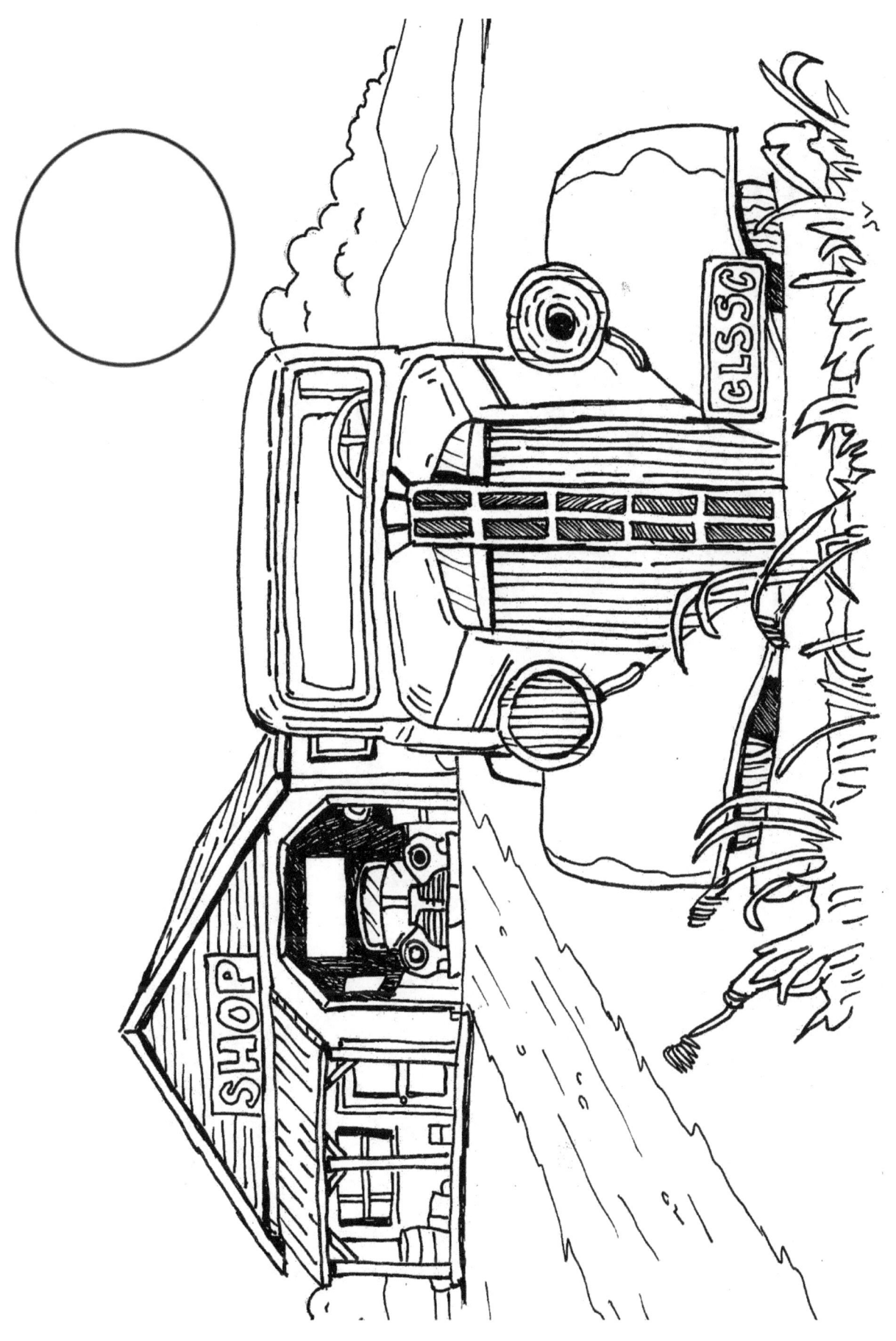

www.ingramcontent.com/pod-product-compliance
Lightning Source LLC
Chambersburg PA
CBHW080551190526
45169CB00007B/2724